GRAPHIC NONFICTION
ELIZABETH I

THE LIFE OF ENGLAND'S RENAISSANCE QUEEN

by
ROB SHONE & ANITA GANERI
illustrated by
TERRY RILEY

The Rosen Publishing Group, Inc., New York

Published in 2005 by The Rosen Publishing Group, Inc.
29 East 21st Street, New York, NY 10010

Copyright © 2005 David West Books

First edition, 2005

Designed and produced by
David West Books

Editor: Gail Bushnell
Photo Research: Carlotta Cooper

Photo credits:
Page 5 – Dover Books
Page 6 (bottom) – Rex Features Ltd.
Pages 7 (bottom), 44 (bottom) – Mary Evans Picture Library
Page 45 – Robert Harding Picture Library

Library of Congress Cataloging-in-Publication Data

Shone, Rob.
　　Elizabeth I : the life of England's Renaissance queen / by Rob Shone & Anita Ganeri—1st ed.
　　p. cm. — (Graphic nonfiction)
　　Includes index.
　　ISBN 1-4042-0246-3 (lib. bdg.)
　　1. Elizabeth I, Queen of England, 1533–1603—Juvenile literature. 2. Great Britain—History—Elizabeth, 1558–1603—Juvenile literature. 3. Queens—Great Britain—Biography—Juvenile literature. I. Ganeri, Anita, 1961– II. Title. III. Series.

　　DA355.S47 2005
　　942.05'5'092—dc22

　　　　　　　　　　　　　　　　　　2004014143

Manufactured in U.S.A.

CONTENTS

WHO'S WHO

Elizabeth I
(1533–1603) Daughter of Henry VIII and Anne Boleyn. Queen of England from 1558. Her reign was followed by James VI of Scotland, who was James I of England.

Robert Dudley
(c. 1532–1588) Earl of Leicester. English courtier and favorite of Elizabeth I. One of the first to be appointed to her Privy Council.

Sir William Cecil
(1520–1598) English statesman and chief adviser to Elizabeth I. He served her faithfully for 40 years, first as secretary and later as lord treasurer. His son Robert took over after his death.

Sir Francis Walsingham
(c. 1530–1590) An English courtier, politician, and strict Protestant. Through his spies, Walsingham helped to protect Elizabeth from Catholic plots.

Mary Stuart
(1542–1587) Also called Mary, Queen of Scots. Mary had a strong claim to the English throne. Elizabeth I was convinced to have her executed in 1587.

Robert Devereux
(1566–1601) Earl of Essex and Robert Dudley's stepson. He was an English courtier, favored for a while by Elizabeth, but later executed for treason.

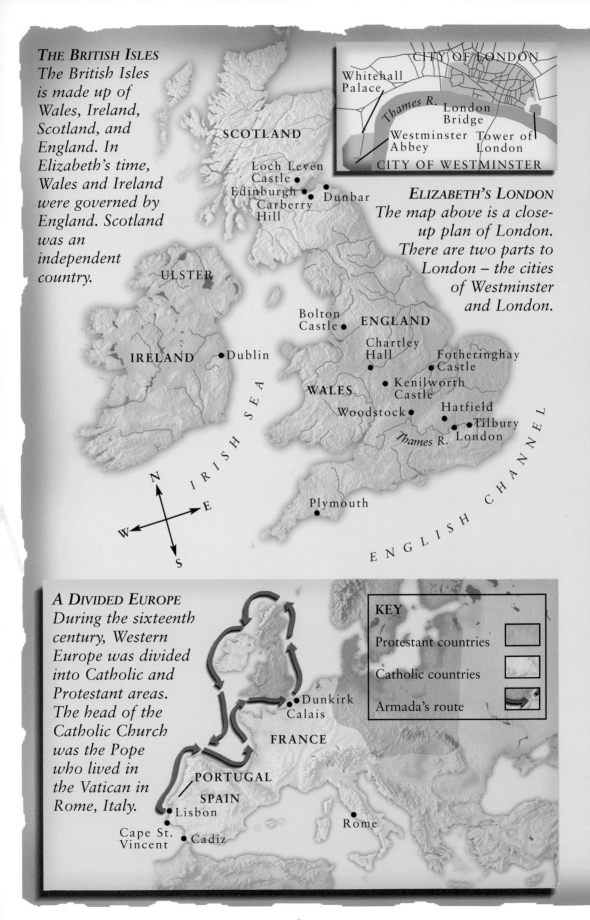

THE BRITISH ISLES
The British Isles is made up of Wales, Ireland, Scotland, and England. In Elizabeth's time, Wales and Ireland were governed by England. Scotland was an independent country.

CITY OF LONDON

Whitehall Palace

Thames R.

London Bridge

Westminster Abbey

Tower of London

CITY OF WESTMINSTER

ELIZABETH'S LONDON
The map above is a close-up plan of London. There are two parts to London – the cities of Westminster and London.

SCOTLAND

Loch Leven Castle

Edinburgh

Carberry Hill

Dunbar

ULSTER

Bolton Castle

ENGLAND

Chartley Hall

Fotheringhay Castle

IRELAND

Dublin

Kenilworth Castle

WALES

Woodstock

Hatfield

Tilbury

London

Thames R.

IRISH SEA

N E W S

Plymouth

ENGLISH CHANNEL

A DIVIDED EUROPE
During the sixteenth century, Western Europe was divided into Catholic and Protestant areas. The head of the Catholic Church was the Pope who lived in the Vatican in Rome, Italy.

KEY

Protestant countries

Catholic countries

Armada's route

Dunkirk

Calais

FRANCE

PORTUGAL

SPAIN

Lisbon

Rome

Cape St. Vincent

Cadiz

ELIZABETH'S WORLD

In the sixteenth century, Spain, France, Portugal, and England fought for control in Europe. In 1558, Elizabeth Tudor became Queen Elizabeth I of England during these power struggles. Elizabeth was clever, shrewd, and ruthless. She established herself as one of England's greatest rulers.

RELIGION

During the reign of Elizabeth's father, Henry VIII (1509–1547), England broke away from the Catholic Church. Henry made himself head of the Church of England and England became Protestant. Most of Europe remained Catholic. Elizabeth's half sister, Mary (reigned 1553–1558), wanted to make England Catholic again. In 1554, she married Philip II of Spain who was strongly Catholic. Protestants were often treated poorly. When Mary died in 1558, the throne passed to Elizabeth, who made England Protestant again.

THE FAERY QUEEN
It was very unusual for a woman in the sixteenth century to not be married, and even more so for a queen to rule alone.

ROYAL MARRIAGES
In Elizabeth's time, marriage between the royal families of different countries was a good way of making political allies. Everyone expected Elizabeth to marry and have a child who would rule after she died. Despite great pressure from her ministers and several marriage proposals, Elizabeth chose to stay single. She once said of her duty as queen, "I am already bound unto a husband which is the Kingdom of England."

THE MEN WHO WOULD BE KING
Elizabeth I had many offers of marriage. Below is a list of some of her admirers.

Adolphus, the Duke of Holstein
The Earl of Arran
The Earl of Arundel
Archduke Charles
Robert Dudley
King Eric of Sweden
Francis, Duke of Alençon
Henry, Duke of Anjou
Philip II of Spain
Sir William Pickering

THE ROYAL HOUSE OF TUDOR

The age of the Tudors began on August 22, 1485, when nobleman Henry Tudor defeated King Richard III at the Battle of Bosworth in central England. He then became King Henry VII.

KING HENRY VIII

When Henry VII died in 1509, his son became Henry VIII. Henry VIII is most famous for having six wives. He and his first wife, Catherine of Aragon, had a daughter, Mary, but he wanted a son and heir. England was a Catholic country, and the Pope would not grant Henry a divorce so that he could marry again. Henry broke away from the Catholic Church, divorced Catherine, and married Anne Boleyn. In 1533, Anne gave birth to a girl, Elizabeth. Furious, Henry had Anne beheaded in 1536. Henry's third wife, Jane Seymour, finally gave him a boy. When Henry died in 1547, his nine-year-old son became King Edward VI.

Henry VII
1457–1509
crowned king, 1485

Henry VIII
1491–1547
crowned king, 1509

Edward VI
1537–1553
crowned king, 1547

Mary I
1516–1558
crowned queen, 1553

Elizabeth I
1533–1603
crowned queen, 1559

HAMPTON COURT
Hampton Court was one of King Henry VIII's favorite palaces.

Anne Boleyn (c. 1501–1536) was Henry VIII's second wife and the first that he had executed.

ELIZABETH'S EARLY LIFE

As a child, Elizabeth was very close to her brother, Edward, and her sister, Mary. After her mother's death, Elizabeth was brought up by teachers and governesses at Hatfield House in Hertfordshire. She learned Latin, Greek, and several other languages. When she became queen, her good education proved very useful.

WILLIAM SHAKESPEARE

The famous playwright William Shakespeare (1564–1616) began writing at the end of Elizabeth's reign.

DRESSING IN STYLE
At court, Elizabeth lived in luxury and liked to entertain in style. She loved to wear beautiful, jewel-covered clothes made from velvet, silk, and satin. Here is a guide to the items of clothing shown on pages 24/25.

*1 **Farthingale** A petticoat stiffened with hoops of twisted fabric, rushes, whalebone, or wire.*
*2 **Rowle** A padded cloth worn around the waist underneath the gown.*
*3 **Kirtle** A skirt or dress.*
*4 **Forepart** A colorful piece of cloth sewn onto the front of the kirtle.*
*5 **Partlet** A short, embroidered shirt that buttoned up under an armpit.*

A GOLDEN AGE

Elizabeth's reign was seen as a golden age for England. It was a period in which the arts flourished. The first theaters, or playhouses, opened in London during the late 1500s. People went to see plays by William Shakespeare, Thomas Kyd, and Christopher Marlowe. Musicians like Thomas Tallis and William Byrd wrote religious music. Poets like Edmund Spenser had their poems published for everyone to read.

ELIZABETH I
THE LIFE OF ENGLAND'S RENAISSANCE QUEEN

LONDON, APRIL 28, 1603. A HEARSE MOVES SLOWLY THROUGH THE STREETS. IT CARRIES THE BODY OF ELIZABETH I, QUEEN OF ENGLAND. ON TOP OF THE COFFIN LIES A WAX FIGURE OF THE QUEEN DRESSED IN HER CEREMONIAL ROBES.

THE PEOPLE OF LONDON SOB OUT LOUD AS THE LONG FUNERAL MARCH PASSES BY.

THE SAD PARADE FINALLY STOPS AT WESTMINSTER ABBEY, THE HOME OF THE ROYAL TUDOR TOMB.

MARCH 18, 1554. ALMOST HALF A CENTURY EARLIER, THE 20-YEAR-OLD PRINCESS, ELIZABETH TUDOR, MAKES A MORE DANGEROUS JOURNEY.

SHE IS ARRESTED AND TAKEN ALONG THE RIVER THAMES, UNDER OLD LONDON BRIDGE, THROUGH TRAITORS' GATE...

ELIZABETH HAS HER OLD GOVERNESS, KATHERINE ASHLEY, WITH HER.

...AND INTO THE TOWER OF LONDON, ENGLAND'S FORTLIKE PRISON.

THE PRINCESS IS TAKEN TO HER NEW HOME IN THE BELL TOWER.

9

THE TWO WOMEN ARE CONSTANTLY WATCHED.

CAW! CAW!

IT IS A SORRY SIGHT TO SEE THE PRINCESS IMPRISONED FOR CONSPIRACY.

DO YOU THINK SHE IS A TRAITOR?

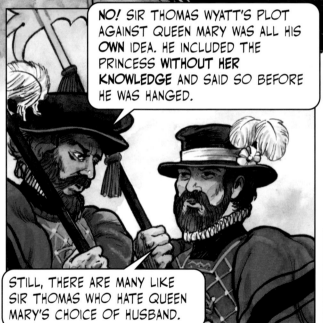

NO! SIR THOMAS WYATT'S PLOT AGAINST QUEEN MARY WAS ALL HIS **OWN** IDEA. HE INCLUDED THE PRINCESS **WITHOUT HER KNOWLEDGE** AND SAID SO BEFORE HE WAS HANGED.

STILL, THERE ARE MANY LIKE SIR THOMAS WHO HATE QUEEN MARY'S CHOICE OF HUSBAND.

TRUE. SURELY, THERE MUST BE AN ENGLISH NOBLE FIT TO RULE BY HER SIDE! WHEN THIS SPANISH PRINCE PHILIP MARRIES THE QUEEN HE WILL BRING NOTHING BUT **TROUBLE** AND **FOREIGN INTERFERENCE!**

WHY DID SIR THOMAS NAME ME IN HIS CONSPIRACY? IT WAS FOOLISH ENOUGH TO TRY TO STOP MY SISTER'S MARRIAGE...

BUT THEN TO WANT ME MARRIED TO THE **EARL OF DEVON!** IT MADE IT SEEM AS IF I WANTED THE THRONE **FOR MYSELF!***

MY LADY PRINCESS, I AM SURE WISE HEADS WILL SOON SEE SENSE AND PROVE YOUR INNOCENCE.

*MARY FEARED THAT A MARRIAGE BETWEEN THE PROTESTANT EARL AND ELIZABETH MIGHT LEAD TO THE ENGLISH PROTESTANTS MAKING ELIZABETH QUEEN.

LOOK, MY LADY! ISN'T THAT MASTER ROBERT DUDLEY, YOUR OLD SCHOOLMATE?

YES. HIS FATHER, THE DUKE OF NORTHUMBERLAND, TRIED TO SEIZE THE CROWN. LIKE ME, HE IS UNDER SUSPICION.

HE WALKS ACROSS TOWER GREEN, WHERE MY MOTHER WAS EXECUTED. EVERY DAY, I WONDER IF THAT WILL BE MY FATE, TOO.

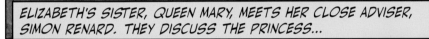

ELIZABETH'S SISTER, QUEEN MARY, MEETS HER CLOSE ADVISER, SIMON RENARD. THEY DISCUSS THE PRINCESS...

MADAM, SHE IS A DANGER TO THE THRONE, THE CATHOLIC CAUSE, **AND YOUR MARRIAGE!** WHILE SHE LIVES, ALL THE TRAITORS AND PROTESTANTS IN THE LAND WILL FLOCK TO HER. **YOU MUST PUT AN END TO HER LIFE.**

BESIDES, I HAVE ALREADY HAD ONE MEMBER OF MY FAMILY BEHEADED.* I AM IN NO GREAT HURRY TO BEHEAD A SECOND.

I DO SUSPECT HER OF TREASON. BUT I CANNOT PROVE IT.

NO, I WILL SEND HER AWAY FROM LONDON AND OUT OF THE HEARTS AND MINDS OF THE PEOPLE.

HIS MAJESTY PRINCE PHILIP HAS STRONGLY ADVISED ME AGAINST A TRIAL. SHE IS TOO POPULAR WITH THE PEOPLE.

*IN 1553, MARY HAD HER COUSIN LADY JANE GREY EXECUTED FOR PLAYING A PART IN NORTHUMBERLAND'S PLOT.

AFTER THREE MONTHS, ELIZABETH IS FREED FROM THE TOWER. SHE IS SENT TO LIVE IN THE CRAMPED GATEHOUSE OF WOODSTOCK MANOR, A RUIN IN THE OXFORDSHIRE COUNTRYSIDE. HER KEEPER IS SIR HENRY BEDINGFIELD.

WHY AM I GUARDED SO CLOSELY, SIR HENRY?

TO PROTECT THE QUEEN FROM YOU, MY LADY, AND TO PROTECT YOU FROM THE **ASSASSIN'S KNIFE.**

TO ELIZABETH'S GREAT SADNESS, KATHERINE ASHLEY IS NOT ALLOWED TO SEE HER. BUT SHE DOES HAVE HER WELSH NURSEMAID, BLANCHE PARRY, FOR COMPANY. THE TWO WOMEN SPEND THE EVENINGS TALKING AND SEWING.

OUCH! MY FINGER!

HAS THE QUEEN SENT THE BOOKS YOU ASKED FOR, MY LADY?

NO. SHE HAS NOT EVEN ANSWERED MY LETTERS.

NOW THAT SHE IS MARRIED LIFE MAY BECOME EASIER FOR YOU.* AFTER ALL, PHILIP DID HELP TO FREE YOU FROM THE TOWER.

*MARY MARRIED PHILIP IN JULY 1554. IN 1556 HE BECAME KING PHILIP II OF SPAIN.

ONE DAY PHILIP WILL EXPECT A FAVOR IN RETURN. ONLY MY SISTER CAN HELP ME THIS TIME.

ALTHOUGH SHE IS SAFER THAN BEING IN THE TOWER, ELIZABETH IS STILL UNDER SUSPICION. SHE SCRATCHES A RHYME ON A WINDOWPANE, USING A DIAMOND RING.

"MUCH SUSPECTED BY ME, NOTHING PROVED CAN BE."

WHILE ELIZABETH IS AT WOODSTOCK MANOR, HER SISTER, MARY, IS BURNING HERETICS.

MADAM, YOUR DEALINGS WITH THE PROTESTANTS ARE MAKING YOU **UNPOPULAR.**

MY LORD PHILIP, TO ME PROTESTANTS AND HERETICS ARE **ONE AND THE SAME!** I WILL FORCE THIS LAND BACK TO THE TRUE **CATHOLIC FAITH!**

WITH EVERY HERETIC MARY BURNS, ELIZABETH BECOMES MORE POPULAR.

IN THE SPRING OF 1555, ELIZABETH IS ALLOWED TO LEAVE WOODSTOCK MANOR. SHE GOES TO LIVE QUIETLY AT HATFIELD HOUSE IN HERTFORDSHIRE, HER CHILDHOOD HOME.

NOVEMBER 17, 1558. ELIZABETH IS IN THE GROUNDS OF HATFIELD'S GREAT PARK. SHE HAS VISITORS.

YOUR MAJESTY, YOUR SISTER, THE QUEEN, IS DEAD. YOU ARE NOW QUEEN.

THIS IS THE LORD'S DOING AND MOST MARVELOUS IN OUR EYES.

THE NEXT FEW DAYS ARE A WHIRL OF ACTIVITY. THERE IS A STEADY STREAM OF FOREIGN REPRESENTATIVES, AMBASSADORS, COURTIERS, AND NOBLES TO MEET.

AMONG THOSE SWEARING THEIR LOYALTY IS AN OLD FRIEND...

I SHALL MAKE YOU MY MASTER OF HORSE.*

YOUR MAJESTY!

ROBERT DUDLEY! A FITTING ENTRANCE!

*THE MASTER OF HORSE TAKES CARE OF THE ROYAL STABLES.

ON NOVEMBER 23, THE NEW QUEEN LEAVES HATFIELD FOR LONDON WITH OVER 1,000 COURTIERS.

CHEERING CROWDS LINE THE ROUTE SHE TAKES. AT THE TOWER OF LONDON SHE MEETS ITS LIEUTENANT. IT IS HER FORMER JAILER, SIR HENRY BEDINGFIELD.

I THANK YOU, SIR HENRY, FOR YOUR SERVICES TO THE LATE QUEEN. BUT I DO NOT NEED THEM. YOU MAY GO.

GOD FORGIVE YOU THE PAST, AS I DO. BUT IF EVER I HAVE A PRISONER WHO NEEDS TO BE SECURELY GUARDED, I WILL **SEND HIM TO YOU!**

THROUGHOUT THE WINTER ELIZABETH IS BUSY. SHE IS KEEN TO STAY IN THE PUBLIC EYE.

ON JANUARY 15, 1559, ELIZABETH'S CORONATION IS HELD IN WESTMINSTER ABBEY. ELIZABETH TUDOR IS CROWNED QUEEN ELIZABETH I OF ENGLAND.

14

ELIZABETH AND HER PRIVY COUNCIL BEGIN THE TASK OF GOVERNING THE COUNTRY. HER CHIEF ADVISER IS SIR WILLIAM CECIL.

THE COUNTRY HAS BEEN **RUINED** BY THE KING OF SPAIN. HE USED THE TREASURY TO PAY FOR HIS FOREIGN WARS.

LACK OF WORK IS DRIVING THE POOR FROM THE COUNTRYSIDE TO THE CITIES. THERE THEY ARE DYING OF HUNGER IN THE STREETS OR TURNING TO CRIME.

OUR ARMY IS WEAK AND OUR NAVY IS MADE OF ROTTING SHIPS. IF EITHER FRANCE OR SCOTLAND DECLARED WAR NOW, **WE WOULD BE BEATEN!**

BUT THERE ARE ALSO DANGERS CLOSER TO HOME. MARY CREATED SUCH HATRED BETWEEN CATHOLICS AND PROTESTANTS THAT BEFORE TOO LONG **ENGLISHMAN WILL BE AT WAR WITH ENGLISHMAN!**

OUR PATH IS CLEAR. WE MUST STOP THE THREAT OF WAR. THE POOR MUST BE CARED FOR AND THE CRIMINALS PUNISHED. WE MUST REFILL OUR TREASURY AND REBUILD OUR ARMY AND NAVY.

FIRST, WE MUST HEAL THE HARM MY SISTER HAS DONE TO THE CHURCH. ALL **ENGLAND** MUST KNOW WHERE IT STANDS IN MATTERS OF **CHURCH AND STATE.**

THAT MAY, PARLIAMENT PASSES LAWS THAT MAKE ELIZABETH "SUPREME GOVERNOR" OF THE CHURCH. THEY ALSO ESTABLISH HOW CHURCH SERVICES SHOULD BE HELD. BOTH CATHOLICS AND PROTESTANTS HAVE TO LIVE WITH THE NEW RULES. BY 1560, TREATIES WITH FRANCE AND SCOTLAND HAVE BEEN SIGNED. THINGS SEEM TO BE GOING WELL. THEN, IN OCTOBER 1562, ELIZABETH CATCHES SMALLPOX...

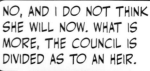

THE QUEEN IS AT HAMPTON COURT NEAR LONDON WHEN SHE FALLS ILL. AT FIRST, SHE THINKS IT IS A CHILL. SIX DAYS LATER, SHE CANNOT SPEAK AND FALLS INTO A COMA.

THE QUEEN IS GRAVELY ILL. I FEAR SHE WILL NOT LAST THE NIGHT.

HAS SHE NAMED A SUCCESSOR, CECIL?

NO, AND I DO NOT THINK SHE WILL NOW. WHAT IS MORE, THE COUNCIL IS DIVIDED AS TO AN HEIR.

LATER THAT NIGHT...

MY LORDS, ALL IS NOT LOST!

WITH LORD HUNSDON IS DOCTOR BURCOT, A WELL-KNOWN PHYSICIAN.

TAKE ME TO HER. THERE MAY STILL BE TIME.

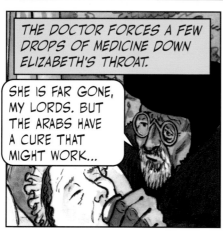

THE DOCTOR FORCES A FEW DROPS OF MEDICINE DOWN ELIZABETH'S THROAT.

SHE IS FAR GONE, MY LORDS. BUT THE ARABS HAVE A CURE THAT MIGHT WORK...

THE QUEEN IS WRAPPED IN A RED FLANNEL CLOTH AND PLACED ON A BED BY THE FIRE.

ALL WE CAN DO NOW IS WAIT.

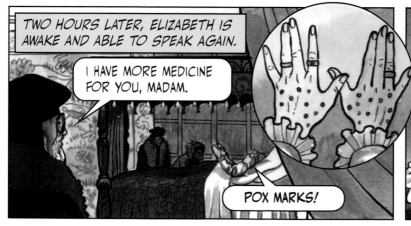

TWO HOURS LATER, ELIZABETH IS AWAKE AND ABLE TO SPEAK AGAIN.

I HAVE MORE MEDICINE FOR YOU, MADAM.

POX MARKS!

BUT THE DANGER IS PAST. SOON THE SPOTS WILL DRY AND THE SCABS WILL FALL OFF.

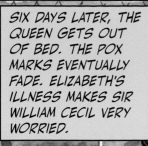

SIX DAYS LATER, THE QUEEN GETS OUT OF BED. THE POX MARKS EVENTUALLY FADE. ELIZABETH'S ILLNESS MAKES SIR WILLIAM CECIL VERY WORRIED.

IF SHE HAD DIED WITHOUT NAMING AN HEIR, ENGLAND WOULD HAVE BEEN THROWN INTO **TOTAL CONFUSION.**

WE SHOULD BE THANKFUL FOR OUR GOOD FORTUNE AND THE QUEEN'S RECOVERY, DUDLEY.

IT IS NOT **RIGHT** FOR A QUEEN TO STAY UNMARRIED. WE MUST FIND A HUSBAND FOR HER.

HOW CAN A **MERE WOMAN** CARRY THE LOAD OF ROYAL DUTY ALONE? SHE NEEDS A MAN BY HER SIDE TO GUIDE HER.

IF SHE DOES NOT MARRY, FOREIGN RULERS WILL THINK THAT OUR COUNTRY IS WEAK.

THE KINGDOM WILL NOT BE SAFE UNTIL THE QUEEN IS **MARRIED** AND HAS **A CHILD.**

IN 1562, ELIZABETH IS NOT THE ONLY QUEEN IN THE BRITISH ISLES. THE YEAR BEFORE, HER COUSIN MARY, QUEEN OF SCOTLAND, HAD RETURNED FROM FRANCE TO EDINBURGH, SCOTLAND. HER YOUNG HUSBAND, KING FRANCIS, HAD DIED. SHE IS 19, A WIDOW, AND WANTS ANOTHER HUSBAND!

MARRIAGE TALKS HAVE STARTED BETWEEN MARY AND DON CARLOS, THE SON OF KING PHILIP OF SPAIN.

IN ENGLAND, ELIZABETH HEARS OF MARY'S PLAN TO MARRY DON CARLOS.

THIS MARRIAGE COULD HARM ENGLAND, SIR WILLIAM.

MARY BELIEVES SHE HAS A CLAIM TO MY THRONE. AND PHILIP HAS MADE IT HIS HOLY DUTY TO SEE ENGLAND BECOME CATHOLIC AGAIN.

IF QUEEN MARY HAS HER MIND SET ON MARRIAGE, WHY NOT FIND HER AN ENGLISH HUSBAND?

YES, THAT WOULD SERVE ENGLISH INTERESTS. DO YOU KNOW OF A SUITABLE GROOM?

YOU WIN AGAIN, DUDLEY!

JUST LUCK, MY LORD!

WHAT ABOUT ROBERT DUDLEY? HE IS A PROTESTANT, SO THE SCOTTISH LORDS WOULD ACCEPT HIM. HE ALSO HAS WIT AND CHARM.

A GOOD CHOICE, THOUGH I WOULD BE SAD TO SEE HIM LEAVE MY COURT. MARY WILL NOT MARRY A COMMONER, SO HE WILL NEED A TITLE. THE EARL OF LEICESTER, PERHAPS?

BUT EVENTS TAKE A DIFFERENT TURN. MARY, QUEEN OF SCOTS, FALLS IN LOVE WITH A CATHOLIC ENGLISHMAN HENRY STUART, WHO HOLDS THE TITLE OF LORD DARNLEY. IN 1565, THEY GET MARRIED.

ELIZABETH IS SURPRISED WHEN SHE HEARS ABOUT THE MATCH.

I KNOW THIS DARNLEY. HE IS A YOUNG FOOL. HE WILL CAUSE MARY MORE TROUBLE THAN I EVER COULD!

18

FOR A WHILE, THE YOUNG KING AND QUEEN ARE HAPPY. DARNLEY SOON BEGINS TO SHOW A DARKER SIDE TO HIS CHARACTER...

YOU! MORE WINE!

SHOW YOUR KING SOME **RESPECT**, YOU **BLACK-HEARTED KNAVE!**

IN DECEMBER, IT IS ANNOUNCED THAT THE QUEEN IS PREGNANT. BY THIS TIME SHE HAS GROWN TIRED OF HER HUSBAND. SHE TURNS TO HER SECRETARY, THE ITALIAN DAVID RIZZIO, FOR COMPANY. DARNLEY'S BEHAVIOR EARNS HIM THE HATRED OF THE POWERFUL SCOTTISH LORDS.

A GROUP OF SCOTTISH LORDS MEET...

DARNLEY IS AN **ARROGANT BULLY!**

AND **A DRUNKARD!** I HAVE EVEN SEEN HIM **FIGHTING** IN THE STREETS LIKE A **COMMON TRADESMAN.**

THE QUEEN IS TOO BUSY WITH DAVID RIZZIO TO LISTEN TO OUR COMPLAINTS.

HOW CAN WE GET RID OF THIS **DISRESPECTFUL** CATHOLIC KING AND THE QUEEN'S ITALIAN BOYFRIEND?

THERE MAY BE A WAY.

UGLY RUMORS ABOUT THE QUEEN AND RIZZIO ARE SPREAD THROUGH MARY'S COURT. DARNLEY HEARS THEM, AS HE IS MEANT TO.

MY LORD, YOU MUST **GET EVEN WITH RIZZIO** AND SAVE YOUR **HONOR.** WITH HIM GONE, YOU MAY WIN BACK THE QUEEN'S FAVOR.

OH **YES**, MY LORD.

YOU ARE RIGHT. I WANT HIM **DEAD.** ARE THERE OTHERS WHO THINK AS YOU DO?

LATER...

HE HAS AGREED TO LEAD THE PLOT. WE SHALL SOON BE FREE OF RIZZIO.

GOOD. AND IF THE QUEEN OR HER UNBORN CHILD ARE HARMED IN ANY WAY, DARNLEY WILL BE ACCUSED OF TREASON. THEN WE SHALL BE FREE OF **HIM**, TOO.

MARCH 9, 1566. MARY AND RIZZIO ARE IN HER PRIVATE CHAMBERS.

PLEASE, SIGNOR RIZZIO, ANOTHER SONG.

SUDDENLY, THEIR PEACE IS BROKEN...

JUSTICE! JUSTICE! SAVE ME, MY LADY!

RIZZIO IS DRAGGED INTO A SIDE ROOM...

...AND STABBED 56 TIMES.

AFTER THE MURDER...

WHY HAVE YOU DONE THIS WICKED DEED?

HE HAS SPENT MORE TIME WITH YOU IN THE PAST FEW MONTHS THAN I HAVE!

FOR SAFETY, MARY LOCKS HERSELF IN HER CHAMBER. LATER, DARNLEY VISITS HER.

YOU FOOL! THEY TRICKED YOU INTO HELPING THEM! DID YOU NOT SEE THAT THEY MEANT TO KILL YOU, THEN ME!

WHAT SHOULD WE DO?

YOU MUST GIVE ME THE NAMES OF THE MURDERERS. THEN WE MUST FLEE EDINBURGH AND GO TO THE EARL OF BOTHWELL'S CASTLE AT DUNBAR.

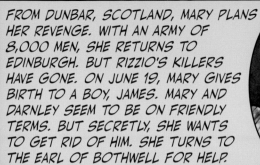

FROM DUNBAR, SCOTLAND, MARY PLANS HER REVENGE. WITH AN ARMY OF 8,000 MEN, SHE RETURNS TO EDINBURGH. BUT RIZZIO'S KILLERS HAVE GONE. ON JUNE 19, MARY GIVES BIRTH TO A BOY, JAMES. MARY AND DARNLEY SEEM TO BE ON FRIENDLY TERMS. BUT SECRETLY, SHE WANTS TO GET RID OF HIM. SHE TURNS TO THE EARL OF BOTHWELL FOR HELP.

THAT WINTER, DARNLEY BECOMES ILL. MARY SUGGESTS THAT HE GO TO STAY AT KIRK O' FIELD, JUST OUTSIDE EDINBURGH, TO RECOVER. HE AGREES AND IS THERE ON THE NIGHT OF FEBRUARY 10, 1567, WHEN...

KERRRBOOOMM!!

OUTSIDE THE WRECKED HOUSE...

HERE! – HERE IS A BODY!

IT IS THE KING, DRESSED IN HIS NIGHTSHIRT. DEAD!

IT WAS NOT THE BLAST THAT KILLED HIM. THERE ARE MARKS ON HIS NECK!

STRANGLE MARKS! THE KING HAS BEEN MURDERED!

MARY VOWS TO CATCH THE MURDERERS, BUT DOES NOTHING.

LOOK! HER HUSBAND IS NOT LONG DEAD, HIS MURDERERS ARE FREE, AND YET THE QUEEN IS **PLAYING GOLF!**

IN MAY 1567, MARY MARRIES THE EARL OF BOTHWELL. THE SCOTTISH LORDS LIKE HIM EVEN LESS THAN DARNLEY. THEY ARE SURE THAT BOTHWELL MURDERED DARNLEY AND THAT MARY IS INVOLVED. THEY REBEL AGAINST THE QUEEN. ON JUNE 15, THEIR FORCES MEET MARY'S ARMY AT CARBERRY HILL.

THE SCOTTISH LORDS WIN. BOTHWELL ESCAPES, BUT MARY IS BROUGHT TO EDINBURGH IN SHAME.

MADAM, FOR YOUR PART IN THE **MURDER,** YOU MUST FACE A TRIAL, ABDICATE, OR DIVORCE BOTHWELL.

I AM YOUR QUEEN AND WILL NOT BE **TOLD WHAT TO DO!** I AM INNOCENT! YOU CANNOT **PROVE OTHERWISE!**

ON JUNE 20, THEY FIND THEIR PROOF.

YOUR LETTERS TO BOTHWELL SHOW THAT YOU **KNEW** ABOUT THE MURDER, AND EVEN **PLANNED IT!**

GASP!

MARY HAS NO CHOICE. ON JUNE 24, 1567, SHE GIVES UP THE THRONE. HER ONE-YEAR-OLD SON IS CROWNED JAMES VI. MARY IS SENT TO THE ISLAND CASTLE OF LOCH LEVAN.

THE FOLLOWING MAY, MARY ESCAPES...

TO ENGLAND...

AND IS IMPRISONED BY THE ENGLISH.

MARY IS TAKEN TO BOLTON CASTLE. SHE IS TREATED WELL, BUT TIGHTLY GUARDED. ELIZABETH HAS THE PROBLEM OF WHAT TO DO WITH HER.

MADAM! YOU WISH TO PUT BACK A CATHOLIC ON THE THRONE OF SCOTLAND! A PROTESTANT COUNTRY?

A COUNTRY THAT REBELLED AGAINST ITS QUEEN...

A QUEEN BLESSED BY HEAVEN, AS I WAS! I CANNOT BE SEEN TO APPROVE OF REBELLION.

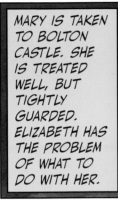

BUT BEFORE SHE CAN WIN BACK HER CROWN SHE MUST GIVE UP HER CLAIM TO MINE.

WILL YOU RECEIVE HER AT COURT?

NOT UNTIL SHE IS CLEARED OF DARNLEY'S MURDER.

IN NOVEMBER 1569, THE CATHOLIC COUNTIES IN THE NORTH OF ENGLAND REBEL. THEY TRY TO FREE QUEEN MARY AND SET HER ON THE ENGLISH THRONE. THE UPRISING IS CRUSHED AND THE REBELS SEVERELY PUNISHED.

SIR FRANCIS WALSINGHAM, A MEMBER OF THE PRIVY COUNCIL, IS IN HIS STUDY. HE IS A HARD-WORKING PROTESTANT — AND ELIZABETH'S SPYMASTER.

THE QUEEN DOES NOT REALIZE IT, BUT THE SCOTS WILL ONLY HAVE MARY BACK TO TRY HER FOR MURDER. THEY WILL NEVER ACCEPT HER AS THEIR QUEEN.

MARY HAS ALREADY PLOTTED WITH THE NORTH IN THEIR REBELLION AND TRAPPED THE DUKE OF NORFOLK IN HER SCHEMES.

SHE AND HER SUPPORTERS WILL BE WATCHED, SIR FRANCIS.

MARY WILL BRING NOTHING BUT MISCHIEF TO THE QUEEN, TO THE COUNTRY, AND TO HERSELF!

1 FIRST COME HER SILK STOCKINGS AND GARTERS, FOLLOWED BY...

MY ADVICE IS **NEVER MARRY!** MY FATHER HAD MY MOTHER AND ONE STEPMOTHER EXECUTED. TWO MORE STEPMOTHERS DIED IN CHILDBIRTH. NO, MARRIAGE IS **DANGEROUS** FOR A WOMAN.

4 A KIRTLE AND FOREPART...

IF I MARRIED AN ENGLISH LORD IT WOULD CREATE SUCH RIVALRIES IN COURT THAT CIVIL WAR WOULD FOLLOW.

5 A PARTLET...

A FOREIGN PRINCE WOULD BE AS BAD...

8 WIG AND MAKEUP...

9 A RUFF...

MY MINISTERS DO NOT UNDERSTAND THAT A SINGLE WOMAN CAN RULE ALONE.

MISTRESS GREY! YOUR **GOWN!**

LOOK AT ALL THAT COLOR AND FINE EMBROIDERY! IT IS FAR TOO GOOD FOR YOU. GO AND **CHANGE** IT!

IN WHITEHALL'S GREAT CHAMBER, COURTIERS WAIT FOR THE QUEEN'S ARRIVAL. AS USUAL, THE AIR IS ALIVE WITH NEWS AND GOSSIP.

HE LEFT IT TOO LONG AND LET THAT QUEEN OF SCOTLAND **WRAP** HIM IN HER **WEB OF LIES.**

SO, THE DUKE OF NORFOLK HAS BEEN BEHEADED. IT WAS **MADNESS** FOR HIM TO THINK THAT MARY WOULD MAKE HIM **KING OF ENGLAND.**

HE WOULD STILL HAVE HIS HEAD HAD HE GONE TO THE QUEEN AT THE START AND CONFESSED ALL. SHE WOULD HAVE FORGIVEN HIM.

LIFE WILL BE MADE HARDER FOR CATHOLICS NOW. EVEN **LOYAL** ONES!

EACH SUMMER, THE QUEEN VISITS THE CASTLES AND MANORS OF HER NOBLES. OVER 1,000 COURTIERS AND SERVANTS TRAVEL WITH HER. IN 1575, SHE DECIDES TO SPEND TIME AT KENILWORTH CASTLE, THE HOME OF ROBERT DUDLEY, THE EARL OF LEICESTER.

THE EARL SEES IT AS HIS LAST CHANCE TO WIN OVER AND MARRY ELIZABETH.

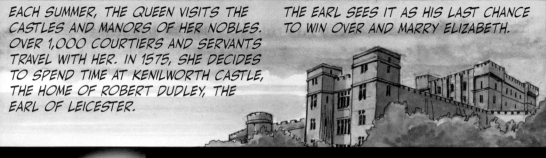

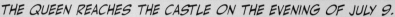

THE QUEEN REACHES THE CASTLE ON THE EVENING OF JULY 9.

THE NEXT 10 DAYS ARE SPENT BEING ENTERTAINED BY THE LOCAL VILLAGERS...

BDUMPH!

HUNTING...

FEASTING AND DANCING...

ELIZABETH KNOWS VERY WELL WHAT LEICESTER WANTS.

WHEN WE WERE CHILDREN, I TOLD YOU THAT I WOULD NEVER MARRY.

WE HAVE BOTH LIVED THROUGH THE TERRORS OF THE TOWER. THAT HAS MADE A SPECIAL BOND BETWEEN US, BUT NOTHING MORE.

DO NOT BE SAD, ROB. WE SHALL ALWAYS BE FRIENDS. WE SHALL GROW OLD TOGETHER, AS FRIENDS.

AH! MY FAVORITE DANCE! COME ALONG, ROBERT!

THE ROYAL PARTY MOVES ON, LEAVING BEHIND A HUGE BILL FOR LEICESTER AND A HUGE JOB FOR THE CLEANERS!

IT WAS JOLLY WHILE THEY WERE HERE, BUT I'M NOT SORRY TO SEE THEM GO. THERE'S HARDLY A **SCRAP** OF FOOD TO BE HAD FOR **MILES** AROUND!

COME ON, THERE'S **WORK** TO BE DONE.

ALTHOUGH THE VISIT HAS BEEN A GREAT SUCCESS, LEICESTER IS DISAPPOINTED.

FRIENDS?! IT IS NOT ONLY THE COUNTRY THAT NEEDS AN HEIR. I DO, TOO. THE EARL OF ESSEX'S WIDOW, LETTICE KNOLLYS, NEEDS A HUSBAND. HMM, I **WONDER**?

IT IS 1579. FOR THE PAST THREE YEARS, LONDON HAS HAD ITS FIRST PLAYHOUSE, OR THEATER.

MY LORDS, LADIES, AND GOOD GENTLEFOLK! WE, THE EARL OF LEICESTER'S MEN, DO THANK YOU!

...THE GIVER OF FRIENDS, THE LORD, GRANT HER, MOST NOBLE QUEEN ELIZABETH!

DODGING YOUR DUTIES, TOM?

JACK! DID YOU ENJOY THE PLAY?

RICHARD EDWARDS HAS WRITTEN A FINE PLAY.

YES, "DAMON AND PITHIAS" IS A STORY OF TRUE FRIENDSHIP.

FOR ALL THE EARL'S WEALTH, HE'S NOT LIKED AT COURT, EXCEPT BY THE QUEEN.

WHY DO THE ACTORS CALL THEMSELVES THE EARL OF LEICESTER'S MEN?

AND SINCE HIS SECRET MARRIAGE TO LETTICE KNOLLYS HE'S EVEN OUT OF FAVOR WITH ELIZABETH.

CLEAN WATER! FRESH FROM THE THAMES!

THE EARL IS THEIR PATRON. HE EVEN PAID FOR THE PLAYHOUSE TO BE BUILT.

FRESH OYSTERS! LARGE SILVER EELS!

RATS CAUGHT!

WILL THE QUEEN MARRY THE FRENCH DUKE, ALENÇON?

INSIDE...

ALENÇON? AH, THE THREE CRANES TAVERN. JACK, ALL YOUR CHATTER HAS MADE ME THIRSTY!

THE QUEEN MIGHT MARRY THE DUKE. BUT WOULD YOU TRUST A FRENCH CATHOLIC AS YOUR KING?

IT'S GETTING LATE! I MUST GET BACK TO THE PALACE. COOK WILL HAVE ME ROASTED IF I'M LATE!

THE SUPPER FINALLY REACHES THE QUEEN'S CHAMBERS.

IT SEEMS STRANGE, SO MUCH FOOD FOR SO FEW MOUTHS.

THE QUEEN HAS A SECRET GUEST. THE DUKE OF ALENÇON IS **STILL** COURTING HER.

YOU CAN COME OUT NOW, MY **LITTLE FROG.***

AH! MY **BEAUTY!**

THE DUKE VISITS ME **UNINVITED!** HE WANTS TO DO HIS **WOOING** FOR HIMSELF!

*ELIZABETH'S NICKNAME FOR THE DUKE.

CECIL, NOW LORD BURGHLEY, AND WALSINGHAM PASS BY THE QUEEN'S CHAMBERS...

OF COURSE, THE DUKE IS HERE **UNOFFICIALLY.** WE MUST **PRETEND** THAT WE HAVE NOT SEEN HIM!

I DO NOT TRUST HIM. HE WILL USE THE QUEEN TO HELP HIM IN FRANCE'S WAR AGAINST SPAIN.

THAT IS WHAT SHE **WANTS** SPAIN TO THINK. PHILIP WILL NOT ATTACK US WHILE HE IS KEPT **GUESSING** AS TO WHAT THE QUEEN **WILL DO.**

ELIZABETH IS 45. THIS MAY BE HER LAST CHANCE TO FIND A HUSBAND AND HAVE A CHILD. ONLY **THEN** WILL THE DOUBT OVER HER SUCCESSOR BE OVER.

YET SHE WILL NOT NAME AN HEIR IN CASE THAT HEIR SEIZES THE THRONE FROM HER.

YES. OVER THE YEARS, I HAVE COME TO ADMIRE THE QUEEN. BUT IF SHE PROVIDES THE COUNTRY WITH AN HEIR, LET US HOPE THAT THIS TIME...

IT IS A KING!

WHILE THE DUKE OF ALENÇON HAS BEEN COURTING THE QUEEN, FRANCIS DRAKE HAS BECOME THE FIRST ENGLISHMAN TO SAIL AROUND THE WORLD. IN 1580, HIS SHIP, THE GOLDEN HIND, RETURNS HOME.

DRAKE HAS BROUGHT BACK A FORTUNE IN CAPTURED SPANISH TREASURE. KING PHILIP THINKS DRAKE IS A PIRATE AND HAS COMPLAINED MANY TIMES TO ELIZABETH ABOUT HIM. SHE NOW WANTS TO REWARD DRAKE WITH A KNIGHTHOOD, BUT HOW CAN SHE DO THIS WITHOUT OFFENDING PHILIP?

BDOOOSHH!

IN APRIL 1581, THE QUEEN AND THE FRENCH AMBASSADOR VISIT DRAKE ON THE GOLDEN HIND, MOORED AT GREENWICH.

ARISE, SIR FRANCIS.

WILL YOU DO THE HONOR, MONSIEUR AMBASSADOR?

ME?!

PHILIP CANNOT COMPLAIN WHEN DRAKE IS KNIGHTED – BY A *FRENCHMAN!*

MEANWHILE, WALSINGHAM HAS AT LAST PLANTED A SPY, GILBERT GIFFORD, IN QUEEN MARY'S HOUSEHOLD.

CATHOLIC TRAITORS HAVE WRITTEN TO HER SEEKING HER SUPPORT. THEY PLAN TO KILL THE QUEEN.

THERE HAVE BEEN MANY PLOTS AGAINST THE QUEEN, MASTER PHELLIPPES. MARY HAS PLAYED A PART IN **EVERY ONE OF THEM!**

WHAT SHALL WE DO, SIR FRANCIS?

SHE HAS BEEN USING BEER BARRELS TO SMUGGLE HER LETTERS IN AND OUT OF CHARTLEY HALL. BUT NOW THAT I HAVE BROKEN HER CODE, WE CAN KNOW **ALL HER SECRETS.**

NOTHING, FOR NOW. SOONER OR LATER, SHE WILL INVOLVE HERSELF TOO DEEPLY IN THESE PLOTS, AND THEN WE **WILL HAVE HER HEAD!**

IN 1586, ANTHONY BABINGTON, A YOUNG CATHOLIC, PLOTS TO MURDER THE QUEEN. BABINGTON AND FIVE OF HIS FRIENDS ARE TO KILL HER. AT THE SAME TIME, THERE IS TO BE A CATHOLIC UPRISING AND A SPANISH INVASION. MARY WILL THEN BE MADE QUEEN.

MARY SUPPORTS THE PLOT IN WRITING – A FATAL MISTAKE. IN AUGUST, WALSINGHAM ARRESTS ALL THOSE INVOLVED IN THE PLOT...

...INCLUDING MARY.

BABINGTON IS THREATENED WITH TORTURE. HE ADMITS EVERYTHING.

THIS IS WHAT COULD HAPPEN TO YOU, BABINGTON!

IN SEPTEMBER, BABINGTON AND THE REST ARE TRIED AND FOUND GUILTY OF TREASON. THEY ARE SENTENCED TO BE HUNG, DRAWN, AND QUARTERED.

NORMALLY, THE CONDEMNED ARE DEAD BEFORE BEING BUTCHERED. BUT NOT THIS TIME...

THEY ARE TRAITORS AND DESERVE TO DIE. BUT NOT LIKE THIS!

THE QUEEN ORDERED THIS.

THEIR SCREAMS ARE TERRIBLE!

IT IS ALL THE FAULT OF THAT WITCH, MARY!

ON OCTOBER 11, THE TRIAL OF MARY, QUEEN OF SCOTS, BEGINS.

I AM NOT A SUBJECT OF THE QUEEN AND AM NOT UNDER HER LAWS. THIS COURT HAS NO RIGHT TO TRY ME.

I WOULD NEVER RISK MY SOUL BY PLOTTING THE DEATH OF THE QUEEN. YOUR EVIDENCE IS FALSE.

YOU HAVE KEPT ME A PRISONER HERE FOR 19 YEARS. ALL I WANTED WAS TO GAIN MY FREEDOM WITH WHATEVER HELP I COULD FIND.

DESPITE HER PLEAS, SHE IS FOUND GUILTY. MARY'S LETTERS TO BABINGTON ARE TOO STRONG A PROOF AGAINST HER. ALL OF ENGLAND CRIES OUT FOR MARY'S HEAD. ELIZABETH IS NOT SO EAGER...

WE ARE BOTH OF US QUEENS, APPOINTED BY GOD. IT IS NOT FOR *ME* TO CONDEMN HER.

THE PRESSURE BECOMES TOO GREAT. ON FEBRUARY 1, 1587, ELIZABETH FINALLY SIGNS THE ORDER TO EXECUTE MARY. IT IS SENT TO FOTHERINGHAY CASTLE WHERE MARY IS BEING HELD.

THE PRIVY COUNCIL ACTS QUICKLY, BEFORE ELIZABETH CAN CHANGE HER MIND. ON FEBRUARY 7, MARY IS TOLD THAT SHE WILL BE EXECUTED THE NEXT MORNING.

FEBRUARY 8, 1587. THE GREAT HALL AT FOTHERINGHAY CASTLE.

LOOK! THE QUEEN'S BODY! IT MOVES!

NO, IT IS THE QUEEN'S LAPDOG.

MARY, QUEEN OF SCOTS, SOON LIES DEAD. THE EXECUTIONER GOES TO LIFT UP HER HEAD BY HER HAIR TO SHOW THE ONLOOKERS. HE IS LEFT HOLDING MARY'S WIG INSTEAD.

HER CLOTHES ARE TAKEN AND BURNED SO THAT NO KEEPSAKE IS LEFT.

ELIZABETH IS OVERCOME WITH GRIEF WHEN SHE HEARS THE NEWS. ALTHOUGH SHE SIGNED MARY'S EXECUTION ORDER, SHE SAYS THAT SHE DID NOT MEAN THE ORDER TO BE CARRIED OUT. HER SHOW OF INNOCENCE DOES NOT FOOL THE CATHOLIC WORLD. IN SPAIN, KING PHILIP IS DETERMINED TO TAKE REVENGE FOR MARY'S DEATH.

KING PHILIP'S PLAN TO USE MARY TO RESTORE THE CATHOLIC FAITH TO ENGLAND IS OVER. HE WILL HAVE TO USE SPAIN'S MILITARY MIGHT TO DEFEAT THE ENGLISH. HE HAS BEEN BUILDING UP HIS NAVY SINCE 1585. NOW IS THE TIME TO USE IT. HE MEETS HIS ADMIRAL, THE DUKE OF MEDINA-SIDONIA.

YOU WILL THEN ACCOMPANY PARMA'S ARMY OF 16,000 MEN, SAILING IN BARGES ACROSS THE CHANNEL AND UP THE THAMES **TO LONDON**.

YOU AND OUR ARMADA, CARRYING 30,000 SOLDIERS, WILL MEET THE DUKE OF PARMA AT DUNKIRK.

BUT WALSINGHAM'S SPIES HAVE NOT BEEN IDLE. THE PRIVY COUNCIL KNOWS OF PHILIP'S PLANS AND IS TRYING TO BUY TIME. IN THE SPRING OF 1587, SIR FRANCIS DRAKE GOES TO SEA.

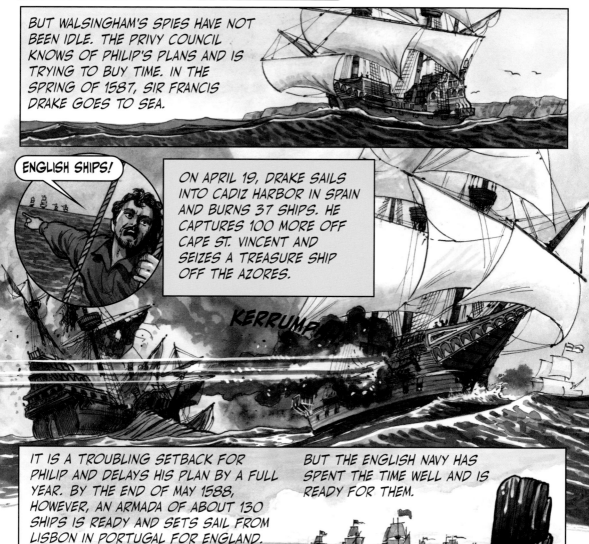

ENGLISH SHIPS!

ON APRIL 19, DRAKE SAILS INTO CADIZ HARBOR IN SPAIN AND BURNS 37 SHIPS. HE CAPTURES 100 MORE OFF CAPE ST. VINCENT AND SEIZES A TREASURE SHIP OFF THE AZORES.

KERRUMP

IT IS A TROUBLING SETBACK FOR PHILIP AND DELAYS HIS PLAN BY A FULL YEAR. BY THE END OF MAY 1588, HOWEVER, AN ARMADA OF ABOUT 130 SHIPS IS READY AND SETS SAIL FROM LISBON IN PORTUGAL FOR ENGLAND.

BUT THE ENGLISH NAVY HAS SPENT THE TIME WELL AND IS READY FOR THEM.

JULY 19, 1588, THE SOUTHWEST COAST OF ENGLAND. THE SEAS AROUND ENGLAND AND WALES ARE BEING WATCHED.

LIGHT THE BEACON! LIGHT THE BEACON!

?!!

BEACON AFTER BEACON IS LIT ALONG THE CLIFFTOPS. THE NEWS REACHES LONDON FASTER THAN ANY HORSE CAN GALLOP...

THE ARMADA IS HERE!

THE ENGLISH NAVY IS MADE UP OF ONLY 36 ROYAL WARSHIPS. THERE ARE OVER 100 ARMED MERCHANT SHIPS AND SMALL CRAFT IN SUPPORT. THE NAVY'S ADMIRAL IS LORD HOWARD. HIS SECOND IN COMMAND IS SIR FRANCIS DRAKE.

THE CAPTAINS MEET THEIR ADMIRAL, LORD HOWARD, ON BOARD HIS FLAGSHIP, THE ARK ROYAL, AT PLYMOUTH.

THE SPANISH ARE MOVING SLOWLY IN A CRESCENT FORMATION. THEY HAVE 20 GALLEONS, LARGER BY FAR THAN **ANYTHING** WE POSSESS, SIR FRANCIS.

YES, MY LORD. BUT OUR SMALL WARSHIPS ARE **FASTER**.

WHAT IS MORE, OUR SOLDIERS AND SAILORS **ARE FIGHTING FOR ENGLAND!**

CAPTAINS, PREPARE YOUR SHIPS. **WE SAIL TONIGHT!**

THE ENGLISH SIGHT THE ARMADA ON SUNDAY, JULY 21. FOR SIX DAYS, THE TWO NAVIES FIGHT. THE SPANISH SAIL SLOWLY UP THE CHANNEL IN FORMATION. THE ENGLISH SHIPS FOLLOW BEHIND.

DRAKE IS ON HIS SHIP, THE REVENGE...

WE **MUST** BREAK UP THEIR FORMATION! ALL WE CAN DO FOR NOW IS HIT THEM AND RUN. THEIR GUNS ARE POWERFUL BUT DO NOT HAVE THE RANGE. OUR GUNS HAVE THE RANGE BUT NOT THE ACCURACY. WE **HAVE** TO GET **AMONGST THEM!**

KERSPLOOSHHH!

JULY 27, JUST OFF THE FRENCH PORT OF CALAIS...

THE TIDE IS TURNING, AND THE WIND IS FROM THE WEST. **PREPARE THE FIRESHIPS!**

DRAKE HAS ORDERED EIGHT OLD SHIPS TO BE FILLED WITH WOOD, TAR, AND GUNPOWDER. AT MIDNIGHT, THEY ARE SET ON FIRE AND ALLOWED TO DRIFT ON THE TIDE TOWARD THE ANCHORED SPANISH SHIPS.

THE SPANISH HAVE DROPPED ANCHOR OUTSIDE THE PORT.

KRACKKKLE!

AS THE BLAZING BOATS BOB TOWARD THE PACKED ARMADA, THE SPANISH CUT THEIR ANCHOR LINES. THEY ESCAPE FROM THE FIRESHIPS AND NO SPANISH SHIP CATCHES FIRE. BUT THE FIRESHIPS HAVE ANOTHER PURPOSE...

IN THE PANIC TO ESCAPE THE FIRESHIPS, THE ARMADA BREAKS ITS FORMATION. SEVERAL SHIPS COLLIDE IN THE DARK. BY DAWN, THE SPANISH ARE SCATTERED.

THE SMALL, SWIFT ENGLISH WARSHIPS CAN NOW DART IN AND OUT OF THE ARMADA, STRIKING AT ITS HEART.

BARROOOM!

KERRRACKK!

ON THE SPANISH FLAGSHIP...

THE ENGLISH HAVE **STOPPED** FIRING, ADMIRAL!

THEY HAVE RUN OUT OF AMMUNITION AND THE WIND HAS CHANGED! **WE ARE SAVED!**

THE SOUTHERLY WINDS PUSH THE SPANISH NORTH. THEY ARE CHASED AS FAR AS THE SCOTTISH COAST BEFORE THE WEARY ENGLISH TURN FOR HOME. THE ARMADA PRESSES ON. IT IS TRYING TO GET HOME BY SAILING AROUND THE FAR NORTH OF SCOTLAND.

STORM AFTER STORM HITS THE SHIPS. WITHOUT THEIR HEAVY SEA ANCHORS, THEY ARE HELPLESS. MANY SHIPS ARE WRECKED AND MANY SAILORS DROWN.

MEANWHILE, THE COUNCIL URGES ELIZABETH TO STAY IN LONDON WHERE SHE WILL BE SAFE. BUT SHE WILL NOT HEAR OF IT. ON AUGUST 8, SHE GOES TO TILBURY, ON THE RIVER THAMES. THERE, ELIZABETH'S ARMY IS EXPECTING PARMA'S MEN TO ATTACK AT ANY TIME. THE NEXT DAY, THE QUEEN MEETS HER TROOPS...

MY LOVING PEOPLE, WE HAVE BEEN PERSUADED BY SOME THAT ARE CAREFUL OF OUR SAFETY, TO TAKE HEED HOW WE COMMIT OURSELVES TO ARMED MULTITUDES FOR FEAR OF TREACHERY...

LET TYRANTS FEAR. I HAVE ALWAYS SO BEHAVED MYSELF THAT, UNDER GOD, I HAVE PLACED MY CHIEF STRENGTH AND SAFEGUARD IN THE LOYAL HEARTS AND GOODWILL OF MY SUBJECTS.

THEREFORE I AM COME AMONGST YOU ALL, AS YOU SEE AT THIS TIME, NOT FOR MY RECREATION OR DISPORT, BUT BEING RESOLVED IN THE MIDST AND HEAT OF THE BATTLE, TO LIVE OR DIE AMONGST YOU ALL.

TO LAY DOWN FOR MY GOD, AND FOR MY KINGDOM, AND FOR MY PEOPLE, MY HONOR AND MY BLOOD EVEN IN THE DUST.

I KNOW I HAVE THE BODY OF A WEAK AND FEEBLE WOMAN, BUT I HAVE THE **HEART** AND **STOMACH** OF A **KING**, AND A **KING OF ENGLAND** TOO, AND THINK **FOUL SCORN** THAT **PARMA** OR **SPAIN**, OR ANY **PRINCE OF EUROPE**, SHOULD **DARE** TO INVADE THE BORDERS OF **MY REALM!***

*TO READ ELIZABETH'S SPEECH IN MODERN ENGLISH, SEE PAGE 45.

EVEN AS SHE IS SPEAKING, THE ARMADA IS BATTLING THROUGH STORMS OFF THE SCOTTISH COAST. PARMA WILL NOT ATTACK WITHOUT THE SPANISH SHIPS. ELIZABETH HAS WON!

ONLY HALF OF THE 130 SPANISH SHIPS THAT SAILED FROM LISBON MANAGE TO RETURN HOME. THROUGHOUT EUROPE, ELIZABETH IS PRAISED FOR HER COURAGE. EVEN HER ENEMY, POPE SIXTUS V, IS IMPRESSED BY HER VICTORY.

IF **ONLY** I WERE FREE TO MARRY. **WHAT A WIFE** SHE WOULD MAKE! **WHAT CHILDREN** WE WOULD HAVE!

IN THE SAME YEAR, ELIZABETH'S OLD FRIEND, ROBERT DUDLEY, THE EARL OF LEICESTER, DIES. SHE TAKES THE LAST LETTER HE EVER WROTE TO HER, PLACES IT IN A SMALL SILVER BOX, AND KEEPS IT BY HER BEDSIDE.

ROBERT DEVEREUX, THE EARL OF ESSEX AND DUDLEY'S STEPSON, IS NOW A COURTIER. HE IS TALL, HANDSOME, LIVELY, AND DASHING. SUCH A MAN QUICKLY CATCHES THE QUEEN'S EYE.

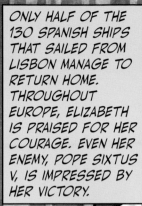

ESSEX IS SKILLED AT FLATTERY, A TALENT THE QUEEN CANNOT RESIST.

HE IS MADE A MEMBER OF THE PRIVY COUNCIL AND ENJOYS GREAT POWER. THE GOSSIPS AT COURT GET TO WORK.

YES, RALEIGH, YOU'RE A SOLDIER. CAN **ESSEX FIGHT?**

THE QUEEN TREATS ESSEX AS IF HE WERE HER **OWN** SON.

I HAVE HEARD HE SEEKS MILITARY GLORY.

YES, AND THEY ARE HARDLY **EVER** APART.

WHAT DO YOU THINK, SIR WALTER?

MOST MEN CAN FIGHT. BUT IS HE A **LEADER?**

BY 1596, KING PHILIP HAS BUILT A NEW ARMADA AT CADIZ. AN ENGLISH NAVY, COMMANDED BY ESSEX AND LORD HOWARD, IS SENT TO ATTACK IT. THE RAID IS SUCCESSFUL AND ESSEX RETURNS A HERO. HE IS NOW THE MOST POPULAR MAN IN ENGLAND.

IN 1599, ESSEX IS SENT TO IRELAND. HE HAS AN ARMY OF 16,000 MEN AND IS ORDERED TO PUT DOWN A REVOLT IN ULSTER. THE CAMPAIGN GOES POORLY. INSTEAD OF GOING NORTH TO FACE THE REBELS, ESSEX STAYS IN DUBLIN. BY JULY, ONLY 4,000 MEN ARE LEFT.

THE REST HAVE DESERTED OR DIED OF DISEASE. AT HOME, ELIZABETH IS GROWING IMPATIENT!

WHY DOES HE SIT IN DUBLIN INSTEAD OF CHASING REBELS, AS HE IS MEANT TO?

ELIZABETH SENDS ESSEX A LETTER, ANGRILY REMINDING HIM OF HIS DUTIES.

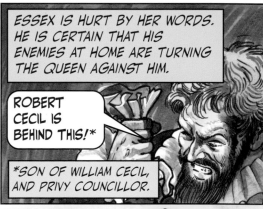

ESSEX IS HURT BY HER WORDS. HE IS CERTAIN THAT HIS ENEMIES AT HOME ARE TURNING THE QUEEN AGAINST HIM.

ROBERT CECIL IS BEHIND THIS!*

*SON OF WILLIAM CECIL, AND PRIVY COUNCILLOR.

ESSEX EVENTUALLY MARCHES HIS MEN INTO ULSTER BUT NOT TO FIGHT. HE GOES TO MAKE PEACE WITH THE REBEL LEADERS – AGAINST ORDERS!

IN SEPTEMBER, ESSEX SUDDENLY LEAVES IRELAND FOR LONDON. HE GOES TO THE QUEEN TO COMPLAIN ABOUT HIS ENEMIES. HE IS ARRESTED AND, IN 1600, BROUGHT BEFORE THE PRIVY COUNCIL. HE IS FOUND GUILTY OF WASTING PUBLIC MONEY, MAKING A TREATY WITH THE ENEMY, AND DESERTING HIS POST. THE COUNCIL STRIPS HIM OF HIS APPOINTMENTS AND PUTS HIM UNDER HOUSE ARREST.

BACK IN HIS LONDON HOME, ESSEX HOUSE, ROBERT DEVEREUX BROODS.

I AM INNOCENT! THIS IS ROBERT CECIL'S DOING. HE WANTS TO SEE SPAIN'S PRINCESS ISABELLA ON THE THRONE! I MUST GET TO SEE THE QUEEN!

AT THE POINT OF A SWORD, IF NEED BE!

WITH THE HELP OF FRIENDS HE BEGINS TO PLOT...

ON FEBRUARY 8, 1601, ESSEX AND 200 FOLLOWERS MARCH ON WHITEHALL PALACE.

WE WILL GATHER SUPPORT AS WE GO. ALL ENGLAND IS WITH ME!

THEIR PLAN IS TO FORCE THE QUEEN TO FIRE HER MINISTERS.

WHERE IS THE SUPPORT ESSEX PROMISED?

THE GATES TO THE CITY ARE BARRED!

ROBERT CECIL HAS KNOWN OF THE PLOT ALL ALONG. HE HAS MADE SURE ESSEX AND HIS MOB DO NOT GET ANYWHERE NEAR THE QUEEN.

ESSEX'S FRIENDS DESERT HIM. ALL ALONE, HE GOES BACK TO ESSEX HOUSE.

SURRENDER, MY LORD!

I WOULD SOONER FLY TO HEAVEN!

THEN WE WILL BLOW YOU AND YOUR HOUSE UP!

ESSEX FINALLY GIVES HIMSELF UP.

THE OUTCOME OF HIS TRIAL FOR TREASON IS NEVER IN DOUBT.

ON THE MORNING OF FEBRUARY 25, THE EARL OF ESSEX IS LED FROM HIS CELL IN THE TOWER OF LONDON TO TOWER GREEN.

THERE, AFTER THREE STROKES OF THE AXE...

SCHUNKT TSCHUNKT SHUNKT

...HIS HEAD FALLS FROM HIS SHOULDERS.

ELIZABETH SHOWS NO REGRET OVER THE EXECUTION. PRIVATELY, SHE MOURNS HER LOSS. SHE IS 67 AND FEELING HER AGE.

THEY HAVE ALL GONE. LEICESTER, BURGHLEY, AND WALSINGHAM. KATHERINE ASHLEY AND BLANCHE PARRY. THE DUKE OF ALENÇON AND NOW ESSEX. EVEN MY ENEMIES, MARY, POPE SIXTUS, AND KING PHILIP ARE DEAD. I HAVE OUTLIVED THEM ALL.

IN NOVEMBER, SHE MEETS PARLIAMENT FOR THE LAST TIME.

TO BE A KING AND WEAR A CROWN IS MORE GLORIOUS TO THEM THAT SEE IT THAN IT IS A PLEASURE TO THEM THAT BEAR IT.

AND THOUGH YOU HAVE HAD AND MAY HAVE MANY MIGHTIER AND WISER PRINCES SITTING IN THIS SEAT, YET YOU NEVER HAD NOR SHALL HAVE ANY THAT WILL LOVE YOU BETTER.

IN EARLY MARCH 1603, ELIZABETH BECOMES ILL. SHE WILL NOT SEE HER DOCTORS AND THE ILLNESS GROWS WORSE. SHE REFUSES TO GO TO BED BUT LIES ON CUSHIONS IN HER CHAMBER.

SIR ROBERT CECIL VISITS HER.

MADAM, YOU **MUST** GO TO BED!

LITTLE MAN, YOU SHOULD NOT USE THE WORD **"MUST"** TO A QUEEN! YOUR **FATHER** WOULD NOT HAVE **DARED** SAY IT. BUT YOU KNOW I AM DYING, AND THAT MAKES YOU BOLD.

TWO WEEKS LATER, ON MARCH 21, THE QUEEN IS FINALLY PERSUADED TO GO TO HER BED.

TWO DAYS LATER, THE END IS VERY NEAR...

YOUR MAJESTY, WE NEED TO KNOW...

WHO IS HEIR TO YOUR THRONE?

UNABLE TO SPEAK, THE QUEEN RAISES A HAND AND MAKES THE SIGN OF A CROWN ABOVE HER HEAD. HER MINISTERS BELIEVE THEY UNDERSTAND HER ANSWER. FOR THE FIRST TIME IN 44 YEARS, ENGLAND HAS AN HEIR.

THAT EVENING, ELIZABETH IS COMFORTED BY JOHN WHITGIFT, HER ARCHBISHOP OF CANTERBURY. AT 3:00 A.M. ON MARCH 24, 1603, QUEEN ELIZABETH PASSES AWAY IN HER SLEEP.

NO SOONER IS THE QUEEN DEAD THAN A SAPPHIRE RING IS TAKEN FROM HER FINGER. AS ARRANGED, IT IS DROPPED FROM A WINDOW AND CAUGHT. THE RING IS TAKEN TO EDINBURGH...

AND TO KING JAMES VI OF SCOTLAND.

AND SO AT LAST, I AM **KING OF ENGLAND!**

IN JUNE, 1603, JAMES VI OF SCOTLAND IS CROWNED JAMES I OF ENGLAND. IN 1612, JAMES HAS HIS MOTHER, MARY, QUEEN OF SCOTS, REBURIED IN WESTMINSTER ABBEY. HER NEW TOMB IS JUST A FEW FEET AWAY FROM WHERE ELIZABETH LIES.

THE END

AFTER ELIZABETH

*E*lizabeth died on March 24, 1603. A month later, thousands of mourners lined the funeral route to watch her coffin go past. Even in death, Elizabeth, affectionately called "Good Queen Bess," remained as popular as ever.

THE STUARTS

When Elizabeth died, she passed the English throne to King James VI of Scotland (reigned 1567–1625), the son of Mary, Queen of Scots. In April 1603, he crossed the border to become James I, the first Stuart king of England. James was Elizabeth's opposite – he was lazy, bad with money, and hated crowds. He was so scared of being murdered that he even wore padded clothes. In 1604, he ended England's costly war with Spain.

James I ruled England as well as Scotland for 22 years. When he died, his son became King Charles I. It was during Charles's reign that England fell into civil war.

THE GUNPOWDER PLOT

Although King James was a Protestant, English Catholics hoped that the new king would end some of Elizabeth's harsh religious laws and give them greater freedom to follow their own faith. They were wrong. A group of Catholic plotters, led by Guy Fawkes, decided to blow up the king. On November 5, 1605, the king was due to open parliament in the House of Lords. On November 4, Fawkes was found hiding in a cellar under the House of Lords with 36 barrels of gunpowder, about to light the fuse.

Fawkes and the other Catholic gunpowder plotters were caught, tortured, and hanged. Some of them had been involved in the Earl of Essex's failed rebellion in 1601.

ELIZABETH IN HISTORY

With Elizabeth's death in 1603, the Tudor age came to an end. But Elizabeth's legacy lived on. Under her long rule, England had become a strongly Protestant country. It had also grown from a weak, bankrupt nation into one of the greatest powers in Europe. The extraordinary story of Queen Elizabeth I has inspired many artists and writers and provided the subject matter for films and television programs. Stately English homes from Elizabeth's reign still attract many visitors who want to see what life in Elizabethan England would have been like.

Little Moreton Hall in Cheshire, England, is an excellent example of an Elizabethan mansion. The black-and-white coloring was made by using black timbers on a white plaster building.

MODERN SPEECH

Here is a translation in modern English of Elizabeth's stirring speech to her troops at Tilbury on August 8, 1588 (see page 38).

"My loving people. Those who look after my safety warned me not to come here today, in case any of my enemies tried to kill me. Let my enemies be afraid. I have always depended on God and my people for my strength and safety. And so I have come, as you can see. I did not come for my own pleasure but was determined to live or die with you in this battle. I am willing to die for God, for my kingdom, and for my people. Some may think that I am only a weak woman. But I have the heart of a king, and a king of England at that. The Duke of Parma, the King of Spain, or any prince of Europe will be sorry if they dare to invade my kingdom!"

GLOSSARY

abdicate To give up power.

allies People or groups who support others.

ambassador People sent by a government to represent it in another country.

armada A large group of warships.

arrogant Conceited and too proud.

assassin A person who murders someone who is wellknown or important.

beacon A light or fire used as a signal or warning.

Catholic A member of the Roman Catholic church.

coma A state of deep unconsciousness.

conspiracy A secret plot or plan.

coronation The ceremony in which a king or queen is crowned.

courtier An attendant at a royal court.

execute To kill someone as a punishment for a crime.

flagship The ship belonging to a navy's commander.

galleons Sailing ships used for warfare.

gossip Idle talk about other people's personal business.

governess A woman who teaches and cares for the children of a household.

groom A man who is about to get married.

hearse A vehicle that carries a coffin.

heretic Someone whose views differ from those of a particular religion.

impress To make people think highly of you.

manor A mansion.

passion A very strong feeling, such as love, anger, or hatred.

patron Someone who gives money to or helps another person or cause.

Privy Council The group of advisers of England's king or queen.

Protestant A Christian who belongs to the Protestant church.

rebel To fight against the people in charge of something.

Renaissance The growth of art and learning in Europe between the fourteenth and sixteenth centuries.

revenge Action you take to pay someone back for harm done to you.

smallpox A disease that causes chills, high fever, and pimples.

smuggle To move goods into or out of a country illegally.

successor One who follows another in a position.

traitor Someone who betrays their friends or country.

treachery Being disloyal.

treaties A formal agreement between two countries.

tyrant A ruler who governs in a harsh or unjust way.

woo To seek the affection of someone.

FOR MORE INFORMATION

ORGANIZATION

The British Museum
Great Russell Street
London, England
WC1B 3DG
(+44) 020 7323 8299
Web site: http://www.thebritishmuseum.ac.uk/

FOR FURTHER READING

Bush, Catherine. *Elizabeth I*. Broomall, PA: Chelsea House Publishers, 1987.

Green, Robert. *Queen Elizabeth I*. Danbury, CT: Scholastic Library Publishing, 1997.

Lace, William W. *Defeat of the Spanish Armada*. Farmington Hills, MI: Gale Group, 1996.

Mannis, Celeste A. *The Queen's Progress*. New York: Penguin Group, 2003.

Thomas, Jane Resh. *Behind the Mask: The Life of Queen Elizabeth I*. New York: Houghton Mifflin Company, 1998.

Vennema, Peter. *Good Queen Bess: The Story of Elizabeth I of England*. New York: HarperCollins Children's Book Group, 2001.

INDEX

Web Sites

Due to the changing nature of Internet links, the Rosen Publishing Group, Inc., has developed an online list of Web sites related to the subject of this book. This site is updated regularly. Please use this link to access the list:

http://www.rosenlinks.com/gnf/eliz